Jo Morris is admitted to the list of Specialist counsel and victim's representatives of the Kosovo Specialist Chambers. She accepts instructions to prosecute and defend war crimes and crimes against humanity. She also has years of experience of military justice. She has represented servicemen in Germany, Colchester and in Aldershot. She has an intimate knowledge of the Armed Forces Act and other relevant legislation and her military background gives her an advantage over others when defending servicemen. She is also well acquainted with operational law and the law of armed conflict.

Libby Anderson has represented service personnel in the UK. She has particular interest in how the international law of armed conflict is adapting to the new challenges posed by cyber warfare, drones, social media and open source intelligence, and changes in the geopolitical landscape. She is familiar with the Armed Forces Act 2006 and other aspects of civilian law, such as the Data Protection Act 1998 and the Regulation of Investigatory Powers Act 2000, which affect military operations.

A Practical Guide to the Law of Armed Conflict

A Practical Guide to the Law of Armed Conflict

Jo Morris
BA, MA, PG Dip
Barrister, Charter Chambers

Libby Anderson
BA, MA, PG Dip, LLM
Barrister, Charter Chambers

Law Brief Publishing

Published 2018 by Law Brief Publishing, an imprint of
Law Brief Publishing Ltd,
30 The Parks, Minehead, Somerset, TA24 8BT

www.lawbriefpublishing.com

Paperback: 978-1-911035-61-9

PREFACE

This book is intended to provide a short introduction to the law of armed conflict. The law is believed to be correct at the time of writing; 22nd October 2018.

The existence of a code of conduct governing war is as old as war itself. Civilisations of long standing have accepted that war should be conducted in a war that keeps the impact upon non-combatants to a minimum. The ethics of war is an ever evolving topic however. As technology improves, the arsenal available to fighting forces changes and new weaponry must be considered. War is waged across the world often against unidentifiable enemies who do not share our commitment to reducing the impact of conflict upon innocents. Despite provocation, our responses must comply with the law.

Jo Morris
Libby Anderson
October 2018

CONTENTS

Chapter One   The Treaties   1

Chapter Two   Basic Principles   7

Chapter Three   Legitimate Targets   13

Chapter Four   Protection of Civilians   23

Chapter Five   Detained Persons   29

Chapter Six   Weapons   35

Chapter Seven   Cyber Strikes   45

Chapter Eight   War Crimes   51

Chapter Nine   Responsibility of Service   65
                     Personnel, States and Legal
                     Advisors

Chapter Ten   Jurisdiction Over War   67
                     Crimes

Chapter Eleven	Robotics and Drones	71
Chapter Twelve	Private Military Security Companies	75
Chapter Thirteen	Sexual Violence in Conflict	81
Chapter Fourteen	Liability for the Actions of Allies	87
Chapter Fifteen	Countermeasures	93

CHAPTER ONE
THE TREATIES

Conflict is as old as humanity. Human beings have waged war throughout history. In the modern world, the primary duty of a sovereign state is to defend the population from foreign aggression and that may require the use of force. However, history is littered with examples of the devastation of war with the consequent casualties and destruction of resources and property. An end to war is posited and war ends not.

The mature states of the modern world have accepted that war should seek to mitigate the misery of noncombatants. In fact, this is not entirely a modern invention. A code of ethics governing conduct in war is almost as old as war itself. The ancient civilisations addressed both the justness of war itself and the justification for actions in the course of war. The code of chivalry in arms developed in medieval Europe. These ancient and excellent principles have given way to the drafting of treaties restricting the conduct of belligerent parties. The modern law of armed conflict (hereafter LOAC) has grown from the middle of the nineteenth century.

The first of three early treaties on international humanitarian law (hereafter IHL) was concluded at the close of the Crimean War. In 1856 the Declaration of Paris was signed. At the Congress of Paris the belligerent parties, which included Turkey, France, and Great Britain, agreed not to allow private vessels to capture enemy vessels and bring them before prize courts to be sold, or to permit warships to seize enemy goods on neutral vessels or neutral goods on enemy vessels. Another forty five existing states signed the Declaration.

The Geneva Convention of 1864 followed, in which the "Amelioration of the Condition of the Wounded in Armies in the Field" was adopted. This set down the principles that "wounded and sick combatants" should be cared for regardless of nationality and allegiance.

The St Petersburg Declaration of 1868 concerned itself with the type of weapons that were acceptable for use. The sixteen state International Military Commission signed a Declaration on 11 December 1868 renouncing the use of any projectile "of a weight below four hundred grammes which is either explosive or charged with fulminating or inflammable substances". This Declaration recognised that warring parties should confine their aggression to military forces and not direct it towards the entire population.

Two conferences were held at the Hague at the turn of the century. One in 1899 (hereafter Hague I) and another in October 1907 (hereafter Hague II). Hague II defined 'belligerents' and set down that combatants who fell should expect to be treated as 'prisoners of war'. It also prohibited the bombardment of undefended localities, demanded a warning in the case of bombardment of defended locations which contained resident civilians and protected places of worship and other historic monuments.

The Geneva Convention of 1906 dealt largely with the condition of the wounded, sick and dead. Those that were wounded or sick must be positively cared for "without distinction of nationality". If they were under the custody of the enemy then they became prisoners of war. Hague II in 1907 applied the principles of Geneva 1906 to maritime warfare, introducing the "hospital ship" to allow for the treatment of those sick, wounded or shipwrecked provided that they were clearly marked.

In 1949, a further conference in Geneva produced four Conventions, replacing 1906 and 1929. The first Convention protects wounded and sick soldiers on land, religious personnel and medical units during war. The second protects wounded, sick and shipwrecked military personnel at sea. The third protects prisoners of war. The fourth Convention protects civilians. Hitherto Geneva had been concerned with combatants but the events of the Second World War had changed the landscape. It imposes obligations that apply to citizens of an occupied territory as much as to citizens at home. It requires humane treatment for all persons in enemy hands and prohibits murder, torture, degrading treatment, and hostage taking.

The Hague Convention in 1954 considered the issue of cultural objects. The Second World War had seen the wanton destruction of sites of national heritage including the Houses of Parliament, Coventry Cathedral, and the *Gedachtniskirche* in Berlin. The Convention defined cultural property as "movable or immovable property of great importance to the cultural heritage of every people" and included "buildings whose main and effective purpose is to preserve or exhibit the movable cultural property". Under Article 4 the "High Contracting Parties under to respect cultural property situated within their own territory as well as within the territory of other High Contracting Parties [...] By refraining from any act of hostility, directed against such property."

A further conference in 1977 added Protocols I and II to the 1949 Geneva Conventions. Protocol I contains protections for the civilian population and sections on the wounded, sick and shipwrecked, "methods and means of warfare" and "combatant and prisoner of war status". Additional Protocol II provides for the humane treatment of non-participants in conflict.

In 1980 the issue of "means of warfare" was considered in the Convention on Certain Conventional Weapons (hereafter CCW). The concern was that some weapons were excessively injurious and had indiscriminate effects. The outcome was a list of Protocols that currently includes incendiary weapons, blinding laser weapons, and mines. Subsequent conventions in 1997 and 2008 considered anti-personnel mines and cluster munitions. The CCW does provide for review conferences.

CHAPTER TWO
BASIC PRINCIPLES

It is critical for members of the armed forces to understand the laws they are governed by when warfighting or peacekeeping. If an act fails to comply with the law of armed conflict then that act is illegal. Every member of the British armed forces receives standard annual instruction and assessments on operational law, in addition to theatre-specific briefings prior to deployment and localised rules of engagement. They are taught the four basic principles of the law of armed conflict: military necessity, proportionality, distinction and humanity. These four principles address different considerations, but are not independent of each other. When planning, the commander should bear in mind military necessity, humanity, distinction and proportionality, balancing the competing demands of these principles to formulate a lawful but effective plan. The planning cycle will take a wide range of factors into account, including the legal framework, all available intelligence reporting and assessments, and the practicalities of available kit, equipment, and other resources.

1. Military Necessity

The legitimate purpose of conflict is to achieve the submission of the enemy at the earliest point in time with the minimum possible losses. The law of armed conflict recognises that sometimes a military end cannot be accomplished without belligerents engaging in some violent or destructive act, that is, committing the act is militarily necessary.

The principle of military necessity permits a belligerent to use only that degree and kind of force that is necessary for the achievement of a given military end. Such force may not be otherwise unlawful. This principle does not oblige engagement in any act deemed militarily necessary, and indeed does not excuse the committal of an unlawful but necessary act; it precludes engagement in any act that is unnecessary.

Taking account of the principle of military necessity prevents a state or individual in breach of the law of armed conflict from arguing that an unlawful act may be committed if it is deemed necessary to achieve the mission.

2. Humanity

Humanity forbids the infliction of any harm or destruction that is militarily unnecessary, and requires the humane treatment of all people, without discriminating due to gender, nationality, religion, race, or political beliefs. This principle prohibits the infliction of gratuitous suffering after the military objective has been successfully achieved. Humanity is therefore linked to necessity in that once a given task has been accomplished, any further suffering is unnecessary. Of particular importance is the humane treatment of those *hors de combat*, such as captured persons (CPERS) or other detainees, the wounded, sick, shipwrecked, and the dead.

3. Distinction

The principle of distinction requires belligerents to distinguish between legitimate and non-legitimate targets with respect to both people and objects. Indiscriminate attacks are prohibited.

Loosely, people can be categorised as combatants and non-combatants. The distinction between combatants and non-combatants is not as clear cut as it seems. Only combatants are permitted to play a direct role, that is, to be directly involved in aggressive actions, in a conflict. Civilians are deemed to be non-combatants and are entitled to certain protections. They lose this protection whenever they take a direct part in hostilities. Merely supporting aggressive actions, for example through working for a defence supplier, does not turn a civilian into a combatant. A combatant who is *hors de combat* is also deemed to be non-combatant and is accordingly afforded protection from attack.

Belligerents must distinguish between legitimate military targets and civilian objects. Certain civilian objects are granted protected status and cannot be attacked. Although civilians are protected from attack by virtue of their non-combatant status, they may be at risk if they are in close proximity to a military target. Collateral, or incidental, damage is governed by the principle of proportionality.

4. Proportionality

Proportionality requires the actions taken to be proportionate with the military advantage expected to be gained from the act. Disproportionate acts, such as actions which result in excessive losses or collateral damage, are unlawful.

Proportionality is a link between military necessity and humanity. If a commander believes that blowing up the fuel store at a dockyard is necessary to achieve his objective, he must weigh the advantage gained against the potential loss to the civilian workforce, civilian population, and property in the area. It may be that the likely incidental damage would not be disproportionate to the military advantage gained by destruction of the fuel store, in which case the commander would not be acting unlawfully. If there is more than one means of achieving the military end, the commander should consider whether one method might carry lesser risk of collateral damage than the other.

It might be that the commander has to accept greater risk to his own forces to bring the attack down to an acceptable level of proportionality. For example, dropping a 400 lb bomb on a suspected command post would achieve the desired military end of destroying that element of the opposition command structure. Equally, sending in a platoon to clear the building and destroy the command post would achieve same military end, albeit with far greater risk to friendly forces. The option of dropping a bomb may therefore seem more appealing to the commander. However, if the command post was in a building next to a school, the lives of hundreds of children, teachers and parents would be at risk from the bomb that would destroy the command post. This is likely to be a disproportionate use of force, and therefore unlawful. The commander might therefore have to put his own forces at greater risk to make his course of action comply with the basic principles of the law of armed conflict.

CHAPTER THREE
LEGITIMATE TARGETS

The fundamental tenet of LOAC is that only certain things and people are legitimate targets. It is expected that belligerents distinguish between civilians and combatants. Combatants are those who are directly involved in the fighting. Members of the civilian population are deemed to be non-combatants and enjoy protection from attack under the law of armed conflict. However this distinction is not so clear cut on the ground. If a civilian is directly participating in hostilities they are also a legitimate target. Anything that is in military use may be a legitimate target. However, proportionality would demand that the military gain be balanced against the harm caused to civilians.

<u>Convention definition of combatant</u>

Combatants are clearly defined by Article 4A of the Geneva Convention III:

1. Members of the armed forces or volunteer corps of any belligerent party to the conflict.

2. Other militia such as resistance groups as long as they satisfy the following conditions:

    I.   they are commanded by a person responsible for his subordinates

    II. they have a distinctive emblem

    III. they carry arms openly

    IV. they operate within the law and customs of war.

3. Members of regular armed forces of a government not recognised by the detaining power.

4. Civilians of an unoccupied country who take up arms to resist the approach of the enemy.

Troops

The members of the belligerent armed forces on either side of a conflict are combatants and have the right to directly participate in the conflict, that is, to attack the opposition and to defend themselves from attack by lawful methods. They are also lawful targets. The exceptions to this are medical personnel and the military chaplaincy. Any unsurrendered enemy combatant can be targeted at all times although any strike would need to be proportionate.

It is a misconception to say that troops that are in disarray having failed in battle cannot be attacked further. Today's defeated soldier will regroup and emerge as tomorrow's threat. A retreating force is a legitimate target of attack unless they actually lay down arms and surrender, thereby rendering themselves *hors de combat*.

Similarly, there is no requirement for hands to be shown. A lawful attack can be carried out by sniper fire or an ambush, the launch of a missile or an air strike.

Non-state belligerent forces

In an age where asymmetric conflict between state actors and insurgencies are increasingly prevalent, due consideration must be given to the status of belligerent non-state actors.

Belligerent non-state actors may be harder to identify as combatants as they are not necessarily recognisable uniformed organisations, using standard kit and equipment. Taking this further, some belligerents may seek to disguise their members as non-combatants in order to avoid attack. Opposition tactics, techniques and procedures may involve *modus operandi* such as wearing civilian dress to blend in with the local population, and caching weapons which can be retrieved from a known location and immediately discarded after use, to assist with disguise as a non-combatant.

Representatives or emanations of the state

Assassinations of political leaders, regardless of their merits, are not lawful unless they are combatants or directly participating in hostilities. Otherwise they are civilians and therefore protected. They may well be prosecuted for war crimes but they cannot be the subject of a targeting killed without due process of law.

Sometimes the political leadership consists of serving members of the armed forces, and so are clearly combatants. Equally it will be possible to argue that a political figure is a legitimate target even when not a serving member of the armed forces because he is part of the military chain of command. Most Ministers of Defence issue orders to the armed forces sufficient to render themselves legitimate targets of attack. The assessment should be on the basis of actual power.

The Queen, even when she is in uniform, should not be a legitimate target because her powers are ceremonial only.

Objects

Article 52 of the Additional Protocol 1 to the Geneva Conventions considers the protection of civilian objects. Article 52.1 is clear - "Civilian objects shall not be the object of attack or reprisal." Looting and other acts of wanton destruction are a war crime. Article 52.2 sets down:

> *"Attacks shall be limited strictly to military objectives. In so far as objects are concerned, military objects are limited to those objects which by their nature, location, purpose or use make an effective contribution to military action and whose partial or total destruction, capture or neutralisation, in the circumstances ruling at the time, offers a definite military advantage."*

Some buildings are military by their nature. For instance, the Ministry of Defence. Many other Government offices would not be, for example the Department for Education has no military function. Such offices could be used to plan military operations or prepare or broadcast war propaganda. This would render them legitimate targets as long as the military tasks were underway at the time of attack.

In fact, buildings of dual use are legitimate targets. Article 52.3 does make clear that "in cases of doubt whether an object [...] is being used to make an effective contribution to military action, it shall be presumed not to be so used." Further, the principle of proportionality would have to be considered. The civilian population must not suffer excessive collateral damage to secure a small military advantage.

Nevertheless, the fact of dual use does not disqualify an object. Most buildings and objects had a peaceful purpose until hostility broke out. Sources of raw minerals and resources service both the military and the civilian population. Strikes against the electricity grid or cyber infrastructure may gain a worthy military advantage but also have an impact upon the civilian population. That does not render them illegitimate. It just means a proportionality calculation must be done.

Similarly, manufacturing sites rarely have a purely civilian purpose. The commercial market can give way to military need. During the two World Wars the entire civilian industry supported the war effort almost exclusively. Car manufacturers can manufacture tanks. Arms dealers can supply the military. Petroleum companies can supply petrol to the military to power tanks and aircraft.

Airports and harbours are usually legitimate targets. They have a civilian purpose but are usually turned over to military use during wartime. Sometimes civilian use continues to a degree, but is severely curtailed. In the case of rogue states, continued civilian use could hide a sinister military operation. Although they are dual-purpose objects, the proportionality calculation is not likely to conclude there is a hide risk to civilians.

Classifying means of inland transport is more complex. Clearly roads and railways are dual-purpose. However, the issue of proportionality would be a stumbling block. Civilians commonly carry on with their daily lives during wartime. Mostly transport is used by civilians to perform basic functions such as going shopping or travelling to work. Trains and buses may be used by both military and civilians, but the cost to civilians is likely to be disproportionately high. Unless compelling evidence existed of military use, this is likely to be a target that carries too great a risk.

Although Article 8.1(a) does refer to "any broad-casting station" when considering a military objective, broadcasting stations and newspapers generally do have a civilian purpose. In peacetime, broadcasting would be their primary purpose and therefore such entities would not be a legitimate target. That may change if they were used during wartime for military purposes. During conflict a broadcasting station could be used for propaganda and as a call to arms. In any event, even if complete military control had been established and the only communication were for military purposes, a proportionality calculation would need to be made.

Defended localities are legitimate targets if the purpose is to strike against resistance or eliminate military objectives. Whole villages can never be a proper target whether it is believed that combatants are hiding somewhere within or not. Bombardment is only permissible if it could achieve a military purpose under Article 52, para 2, Additional Protocol I. Of course, collateral damage will be inevitable but there must be efforts to reduce this and the damage must not be disproportionate.

Further, Article 57 Additional Protocol I requires that an attacking force should give advance warning of any strike in order to give the enemy a chance to evacuate civilians from the area. The only exception is where the success of the onslaught depends almost entirely upon the advantage of surprise. Then the principle of military necessity would recognise that a warning is counter productive and so unnecessary.

This creates thorny problems for a lawful fighting force if a rogue state uses its civilian population as a screen for military activities. Article 51, paragraph 8 Additional Protocol I expressly confirms that the conduct of a rogue state does not excuse an attacker from his legal obligations under international law. This does cause a lawful fighting force extreme difficulties as he faces an adversary who uses LOAC against him whilst being willing to breach it himself.

CHAPTER FOUR
PROTECTION OF CIVILIANS

The protection of civilians flows logically from the fundamental principle of distinction. Only military personnel and objects are proper targets. Therefore a weapon can never be legitimately drawn against a civilian.

A civilian is defined in Article 50.1 Additional Protocol I as "any person who is not a member of the armed forces".

Civilians enjoy a general protection from the dangers arising from conflict (Article 51.1)) and remain protected unless and until they being to act as a direct participant to the hostilities (Article 51.3).

A civilian is protected from any aggression whether in strike or defence. Breach of such protection is a war crime (Article 51.2)). That does not mean civilians must never suffer during hostilities. That is inevitable in a war zone. They may well fall victim to collateral damage in the course of legitimate action. What is prohibited is any intentional targeting of civilians.

The protection covers any act that causes casualty or injury to the civilian population but also applies to any action designed to cause terror (Article 51.2)). Strikes must not have a primary objective of damaging the morale of the civilian population even if the goal is to cause them to turn away from loyalty towards a rogue state. Of course, acts that serve a military purpose but cause incidental terror in the host population are permissible. It is important to note that threats of such acts are also prohibited.

Indiscriminate attacks are prohibited. Article 51.4 defines such attacks as:

1. those which are not directed at a specific military objective

2. those which employ a method or means of combat which cannot be directed at a specific military objective or

3. those which employ a method or means of combat the effects of which cannot be limited as required by this Protocol

Art 51(4)(a) is unhelpful. Very little guidance is provided. However, Art 52(2) defines military objectives, as far as objects are concerned, in this way:

> *"Those objects which by their nature, location, purpose or use make an effective contribution to military action and who total or partial destruction, capture or neutralisation, in the circumstances ruling at the time, offers a definite military advantage".*

The armed forces may be attacked where ever they are. In combat areas, buildings and installations are often occupied by the military and would therefore be legitimate targets subject to the principle of proportionality. Outside of a combat area greater care would need to be taken to ascertain the character of objectives before acting.

Art 51(4)(b) concerns attacks which *cannot* be directed at a specific military objective. This concerns both weapons and their manner of use. As far as weaponry goes, most fighting forces do strive to use precision weapons so that their strikes are effective. However, this section does raise concern about the use of landmines and other similar devices that are harder to aim at specific targets. The United Nations convened a conference in 1980 that adopted a number of Protocols dealing with the issue of landmines and booby traps. Belligerents are required to give warnings to the civilian population of the presence of of such devices. Also prohibited are mines that are laid randomly such as by air strike unless the area is entirely turned over to military use.

Art 51(4)(c) covers that which cannot be limited by the above Protocol. Some means of warfare are such that the effects cannot be limited to directed towards some targets and not others. For instance, bombardment of whole areas which used during the Second World War or any attack which is excessive in effect compared to the military advantage.

Two examples are provided in Art 51(5) or attacks that should be considered indiscriminate:

1. an attack by bombardment by any methods or means which treats as a single military objective a number of clearly separated and distinct military objectives located in a city, town or village [...]

2. an attack which may be expected to cause incidental loss of civilian life, injury to civilians, damage to civilian objects [...] Which would be excessive in relation to the concrete and direct military advantage.

Clearly Art 51(5)(a) seeks to restrict indiscriminate bombardment of whole areas.

Art 51(5)(b) demands the usual balancing exercise between military necessity and the damage to the civilian population.

What is "excessive" is famously difficult to define. Some guidance is provided in the case of *Galic - Prosecutor v Galic* (Case no-IT-98-29-T, ICTY Trial Chamber I). That case defines the test as whether "a reasonably well-informed person in the circumstances of the actual perpetrator, making reasonable use of the information available to him or her, could have expected excessive civilian casualties to result from the attack".

A civilian will only lose this protection if he directly participates in the conflict, that is, becomes a combatant. The immunity of civilians is a condition that is applied very strictly.

"Direct participation" has been held to mean engage in an act of war that is likely to cause actual harm to the personnel or equipment of the belligerent party. A civilian would only lose his protected status as a civilian during the course of committing such an act. However, it should be noted that if a civilian becomes classified as a combatant, even temporarily, they are entitled to prisoner of war status if captured. Once he ceases taking a direct role, and without the need to surrender, he becomes a civilian again and therefore protected. This would not prevent the authorities making an arrest as long as there is compliance with Art 45 which covers the protection of persons who have taken part in hostilities.

A further exception to the rule that civilians are non-combatants is the *levee en masse*. This refers to the spontaneous temporary mobilisation of the civilian population in the defence of a territory not yet occupied, for example in response to an invasion. Participants in a *levee en masse* lose their civilian status and are deemed to be combatants, provided they carry arms openly and respect the laws and customs of war.

CHAPTER FIVE
DETAINED PERSONS

It is settled law that war should be fought only between combatants, and non-combatants protected. However, there are also rules governing the treatment of belligerents.

The law of armed conflict does not give any particular power rights of enforcement. It restricts instead what can or cannot be done in the course of a conflict. However, detention has been considered to be legitimate as it is within the nature of an armed conflict.

<u>Prisoners of War</u>

Belligerent parties may be captured and interned because of their status as members of the armed forces. They need not stand accused of any specific action or offence; mere membership of the opposition forces is sufficient. LOAC allows this as belligerents are always part of the enemy's potential and the capture and attack of such persons weakens the opponent. However, they are entitled to prisoner of war (POW) status as long as they fall into one of following categories listed in Article 4(A) of the Convention:

1. Members of the armed forces of a Party to the conflict as well as members of militias or volunteer corps forming part of such armed forces

2. Members of other militias and members of other volunteer corps, including those of organised resistance movements belonging to a Party to the conflict and operating in or outside their own territory, even if this territory is occupied, provided that such militias or volunteer corps, including such organised resistance movements, fulfil the following conditions:

   I. that of being commanded by a person responsible for his subordinates.

   II. that of having a fixed distinctive sign recognisable at a distance

   III. that of carrying arms openly

   IV. that of conduct their operations in accordance with the laws and customs of war

3. Members of regular armed forces who profess allegiance to a government or an authority not recognised by the detaining power

4. Persons who accompany the armed forces without actually being members thereof, such as, civilian members of military aircraft crews, war correspondents, supply contractors, members of labour units or services responsible for the welfare of the armed forces, provided that they have received authorisation from the armed forces which they accompany

5. Members of crews, including masters, pilots and apprentices of the merchant marine and the crews of civil aircraft of the parties to the conflict, who do not benefit by more favourable treatment under any other provision of international law

6. Inhabitants of a non-occupied territory who, on the approach of the enemy, spontaneously take up arms to resist the invading forces.

POW status allows a person to be treated in accordance with the standard required under Geneva Convention III and released without delay on the cessation of hostilities.

The Geneva Conventions provide that members of militias and volunteer corps qualify for POW status.

Detention of civilians

Geneva Convention IV does allow for the detention of civilians if their conduct justifies it, under the terms of Geneva Convention III.

Article 78 of Geneva Convention IV provides that "an occupying power [may if it] considers it necessary, for imperative reasons of security" intern civilians. This is clearly confined to those who pose a security risk although those terms are barely defined. Such a person is entitled to the protections of Section IV of Part II of the Geneva Convention IV.

There are limitations upon the length of any such internment because it is conduct based rather than status based. It is not sufficient to say that a person will be detained until "the end of hostilities". The detention of a civilian must be subject to an initial review by "an administrative court".

Practices such as sensory deprivation, sleep deprivation, and the use of stress positions are also prohibited.

CHAPTER SIX
WEAPONS

The use of weapons in the pursuit of armed conflict is permitted but belligerents do not have unlimited choice over which weapons they can use. Some weapons are forbidden by virtue of being specifically prohibited in treaties. Banning a weapon by name and specification has the advantage of precision, but it leaves scope for states to develop new weapons not captured by the prohibition, but which have a similar effect. Other weapons are banned because the consequences of using it would breach the principles of LOAC, that is, military necessity, humanity, distinction and proportionality. Similarly, lawful weapons cannot be used in a way that would result in an unlawful effect. However, there is room for interpretation about the nature and extent of effect. The development of new weaponry and military technology means that questions over the lawfulness of weapons have remained prominent throughout the last century.

Prohibited Conventional Weapons

Conventional weapons are considered to be all weapons other than weapons of mass destruction. LOAC restricts or prohibits the use of certain conventional weapons by means of the Convention on Conventional Weapons 1980.

Expanding Bullets

The use of expanding bullets, often referred to as 'dum dum' bullets, was originally prohibited by the 1899 Hague Declaration. These bullets which "expand or flatten easily in the human body, such as bullets with a hard envelope which does not entirely cover the core or is pierced with incisions" expand upon impact causing unnecessarily serious wounds with the intention of disabling anyone hit. Such wounds might be caused by the sudden expansion of the bullet, or by fragmentation. This offends against the principle of necessity, and as such states customarily regard themselves as prohibited from using expanding bullets under international law, regardless of whether they were a party to the initial Declaration.

Incendiary Devices

An incendiary weapon is 'any weapon or munition which is primarily designed to set fire to objects or to cause burn injury to persons through the action of flame, heat, or a combination thereof, produced by a chemical reaction of a substance delivered on the target', including, for example, bombs, flamethrowers, and use of agents such as napalm. Incendiaries were some of the most contentious weapons of the 20th century due to their use in the 1945 bombing of Dresden and, later, the Vietnam War.

Incendiary and exploding bullets are prohibited as they offend against the principle of necessity by causing superfluous injuries. An ordinary solid bullet would have the desired effect; it is unnecessary to set an enemy combatant on fire in order to disable them. It should be noted that this prohibition only applies to incendiary or exploding bullets intended for use against personnel. It does not prohibit rounds intended for use against materiel targets, even though personnel may be injured. Nor does it prohibit the use of tracer rounds, which can sometimes have an incendiary effect.

The use of other incendiary weapons against military targets is not prohibited. This is subject to the provision that airborne incendiary devices are not to be used against military targets co-located with civilian populations. This rule protects both permanent settlements such as towns and cities, and temporary concentrations such as refugee camps.

Fragmentation Weapons

Although hand-grenades and other similar fragment-ation weapons are not prohibited, it is forbidden to use fragmentation weapons that discharge fragments that cannot be detected by x-rays. Any fragmentation weapon designed to cause unnecessary suffering or superfluous injury is also forbidden.

Laser Weapons

It is absolutely prohibited to use laser weapons which are designed to cause permanent blindness, whether this is the sole intended function or one of a number of functions. This prohibition only applies to damage caused to unenhanced vision. The use of laser systems against optical equipment is permitted, even though the user of that equipment may be rendered blind.

Landmines

The Ottawa Convention 1997 prohibits the use, development, production, acquisition, stockpiling, retention, or transfer of anti-personnel mines. The Convention required states to destroy any existing stockpiles, with the exception of a small number of mines for training purposes. Although the UK is a signatory to this Convention, section 5 of the Landmines Act 1998 provides that members of the UK armed forces will not be guilty of an offence merely by reason of taking part in joint operations with forces of an ally not bound by the Ottawa Convention which deploys anti-personnel landmines.

Anti-vehicle landmines are not prohibited but are subject to a number of constraints and rules set down in Article 3 of the Amended Mines Protocol, as well as being subject to the principles of LOAC.

Anti-vehicle landmines must not be used indiscriminately. They may only be deployed against or used to protect military objectives, and must never be used against the civilian population, even by way of reprisals. They must not cause unnecessary suffering or superfluous injury.

It is mandatory to keep records of the coordinates, dimensions, and nature of any minefields laid to maximise safety and assist with later detection and clearance of mines. Such records, which may be in the form of maps or diagrams, should contain relevant information such as the type of device, number, emplacing method, type of fuse, lifetime, date and time of laying, and any anti-handling devices. Where possible, the exact position of each mine should be recorded.

Where the laying of a minefield is considered necessary, it is of critical importance to consider both the immediate and long term impact of landmines upon the civilian population. Advanced warning must be given of any deployment of mines that might affect the civilian population unless the circumstances make this impossible. Combatants deploying landmines should consider measures such as fencing, signs, or other warnings or ongoing monitoring to keep civilians out of the minefield and minimise civilian casualties.

Anti-vehicle mines must not be designed in such a way that they are detonated by mine detectors. Any anti-handling device must deactivate when the mine deactivates. After the cessation of active hostilities, mines must either be cleared before the area is abandoned, or else responsibility for clearing any mines laid must be handed over to another state.

Booby Traps

The Amended Mines Protocol defines a booby trap as 'any device or material which is designed, constructed or adapted to kill or injure, and which functions unexpectedly when a person disturbs or approaches an apparently harmless object or performs an apparently safe act'.

Booby traps may be used only against combatants. They must not under any circumstances by directed against civilians, nor must they be used indiscriminately. Booby traps should be set up so that there is a 'reasonable prospect' that only combatants will fall victim to them. The military advantage must be greater than any risk to civilians. With a view to protecting civilians and in particular children, it is prohibited to use booby-traps in the form of apparently harmless portable objects which are specifically designed and constructed to contain explosive material, however it is permitted to booby trap existing items such as everyday portable objects. It is absolutely prohibited to construct booby traps using internationally recognised protective emblems, signs, or signals; sick, wounded or dead persons; burial or cremation sites or graves; medical facilities, equipment, supplies or transportation; children's toys or items designed for use by children; food or drink; or kitchen utensils or appliances unless on a military location.

Where there is a risk that civilians may become victims of booby traps, precautions must be taken to protect them, for example, signage should be displayed on a booby-trapped building. The location of all booby traps should be recorded.

Poison, Chemical and Biological Weapons

Poison has been used in conflict for millennia, whether poisoning water supplies, burning pitch, firing arrows dipped in excrement, or deliberately spreading infectious diseases. It is now forbidden to use poison or poisoned weapons in warfare, including the deliberate contamination of water supplies. This primitive chemical and biological warfare has evolved, combining chemical agents and pathogens with sophisticated weaponry.

The Chemical Weapons Convention 1993 defines chemical weapons as including toxic chemicals and their precursors, munitions and devices specifically designed to cause death or other harm through the toxic properties of those toxic chemicals, and any equipment specifically designed for use directly in connection with the use of such munitions. Parties to the Convention undertake never under any circumstances to develop, produce, otherwise acquire, stockpile or retain chemical weapons, or transfer, directly or indirectly, chemical weapons to anyone, to use or engage in any military preparations to use chemical weapons, or to assist, encourage or induce, in any way, anyone to engage in any activity prohibited by the Convention. Further, parties are required to actively destroy any existing chemical weapons and chemical weapons facilities.

The Geneva Gas Protocol 1925 prevented "the use in war of asphyxiating, poisonous or other gases, and all analogous liquids, materials or devices". The regulation of the use of gas in war developed over the course of the last century.

Use of biological weapons was prohibited by the Biological Weapons Convention 1972.

Weapons of Mass Destruction

The United Nations defines weapons of mass destruction as including atomic explosive weapons, radioactive material weapons, and lethal chemical and biological weapons. There are ongoing global efforts to prevent the use of weapons of mass destruction by prohibiting their use but also prohibiting the development and stockpiling of new weapons.

Emerging Weapons

For information on emerging weapons systems such as drones, robotics, nanotechnology and cyber attacks, please see the dedicated chapters below.

CHAPTER SEVEN
CYBER STRIKES

Cyber warfare raises unique issues. The first and most obvious is that of jurisdiction and sovereignty. No single state has sovereignty over cyberspace. Equally, it is difficult to identify that an attack has taken place and cyberspace is therefore difficult to defend. Even when identified, it may not be obvious that an attack is an act of war as opposed to business crime or social activism. Cyberspace has low barriers allowing nefarious online activity to grow. In response to what was perceived as the censorship of Wikileaks, an online activity group launched a series of cyber attacks at Paypal and various credit card companies in revenge for the decisions of these companies to suspend donations to Wikileaks. They were able to do so by downloading a programme from the internet.

However, economic espionage has been used by states before. Hitler's attempt to floor the British economy with foreign currency is an instance in point. More recently, cyber attacks against Estonia in 2007 brought the nation to a standstill in one month.

Cyber strikes require no kinetic action at all. The release of computer viruses would be adequate if they struck at either military or core services databases. The release of the Trojan Horse virus may have been a warlike act of aggression. It is clear that a war crime could be committed by an attempt to cripple a basic infrastructure.

Cyber attacks are particularly nefarious. They raise issues of self-protection and of anonymity. The source of a strike is hard to locate. It can easily be done from obscured locations and hard to identify as an act of warfare at all. Cyber intrusions may be an act of aggression, of commercial espionage, or just domestic computer misuse, for instance "phishing".

Equally, where state actors commit acts of commercial espionage it may be an attempt to cripple essential infrastructure. Normally one would think that referred to utilities services and the like. However, banking and finance attacks would have a similar effect. A strike upon the basis of an economy would have the effect of weakening a nation before a kinetic strike.

The problem of attribution extends even to the timing of a strike. It is possible to release malware and await its activation in the future.

A definition of a cyber attack has been attempted in the Tallin Manual on the International Law Applicable to Cyber Warfare, 2012.

Eight factors were identified:

1. Severity. An operation must result in "damage, destruction, injury or death" rather than "mere inconvenience or irritation".

2. Immediacy. Although delay is perfectly possible with cyber warfare, an act is more easily categorised as an act of war if it's repercussions are felt quickly.

3. Directness. There needs to be a clear causal link between a cyber strike and the consequence of it.

4. Invasiveness. Invasiveness considers the degree to which cyber operations intrude into the target state or it's cyber system contrary to the interests of that state. The experts determined that cyber operations that strike against the domain name of a particular state may be considered more invasive than those operations directed at non-State

specific domain name extensions such as .com. However it was determined that actions such as disabling cyber security mechanisms in order to monitor keystrokes, though highly invasive, would be unlikely to be an act of force.

5. Measurability of effects. Traditionally, the effects of any use of force are highly measurable. The effect is the entire purpose of the strike. In the cyber world, that is not so. Consequences may be far less apparent and more latent. Accordingly, the Tallin experts determined that the more quantifiable the consequences the easier it will be for a State to assess the situation when determining whether the act rises to an act of force.

6. Military character. A nexus between the cyber operation and military operations heightens the likelihood of it being considered use of force.

7. State involvement. The clearer and closer a nexus between a state and cyber operations, the more likely it is that other states will consider them as uses of force.

8. Presumptive legality. International law, like domestic law, is prohibitive in nature. An act that is not forbidden is permitted. For example, international law does not prohibit propaganda, psychological operations, espionage or mere economic pressure per se. Therefore, use of these measures will not be a use of force.

Of course, these factors are not exhaustive.

CHAPTER EIGHT
WAR CRIMES

It has been argued that every violation of the law during armed conflict can be a war crime. War crimes are ultimately only acts contrary to LOAC and there must be accountability both of individuals and states.

However, such a comprehensive definition is unhelpful. Quite apart from anything else, some very serious contraventions of international law, such as genocide, can be committed also during peacetime. Such crimes transcend LOAC.

There is no accepted definition of a war crime. The definition in Article 6 (b) of the Charter of the International Military Tribunal, annexed to the London Agreement from the Prosecution and Punishment of the Major War Criminals of the European Axis 1945, used to be relied upon. That sets down that war crimes include:

> "*violations of the laws or customs of war. Such violations include, but not be limited to, murder, treatment or deportation to slave labour or for any other purpose of the civilian population of or in occupied territory, murder or ill-treatment of prisoners of war persons on the seas, killing of*

hostages, plunder of public or private property, wanton destruction of cities, towns or villages, or devastation not justified by military necessity."

The Geneva Convention does differentiate between grave and ordinary breaches but it is clear that it was never intended to be an exhaustive list of war crimes (Article 85.5) of the AP/I).

Article 8.2 of the 1998 Rome Statute of the ICC provides the most recent definition. Article 8.2(a) confirms the grave breaches of the Geneva Conventions:

1. Wilful killing

2. Torture or inhuman treatment, including biological experiments

3. Wilfully causing great suffering, or serious injury to body or health

4. Extensive destruction and appropriation of property, not justified by military necessity and carried out unlawfully and wantonly

5. Compelling a prisoner of war or other protected person to serve in the forces of a hostile power.

6. Wilfully depriving a prisoner of war or other protected person of the rights of fair and regular trial

7. Unlawful deportation or transfer or unlawful confinement

8. Taking of hostages.

Article 8.2(b) sets down other "serious violations":

1. Intentionally directing attacks against the civilian population as such or against individual civilians not taking direct part in hostilities;

2. Intentionally directing attacks against civilian objects, that is, objects which are not military objectives;

3. Intentionally directing attacks against personnel, installations, material, units or vehicles involved in a humanitarian assistance or peacekeeping mission in

accordance with the Charter of the United Nations, as long as they are entitled to the protection given to civilians or civilian objects under the international law of armed conflict;

4. Intentionally launching an attack in the knowledge that such attack will cause incidental loss of life or injury to civilians or damage to civilian objects or widespread, long-term and severe damage to the natural environment which would be clearly excessive in relation to the concrete and direct overall military advantage anticipated;

5. Attacking or bombarding, by whatever means, towns, villages, dwellings or buildings which are undefended and which are not military objectives;

6. Killing or wounding a combatant who, having laid down his arms or having no longer means of defence, has surrendered at discretion;

7. Making improper use of a flag of truce, of the flag or of the military insignia and

uniform of the enemy or of the United Nations, as well as of the distinctive emblems of the Geneva Conventions, resulting in death or serious personal injury;

8. The transfer, directly or indirectly, by the Occupying Power of parts of its own civilian population into the territory it occupies, or the deportation or transfer of all or parts of the population of the occupied territory within or outside this territory;

9. Intentionally directing attacks against buildings dedicated to religion, education, art, science or charitable purposes, historic monuments, hospitals and places where the sick and wounded are collected, provided they are not military objectives

10. Subjecting persons who are in the power of an adverse party to physical mutilation or to medical or scientific experiments of any kind which are neither justified by the medical, dental or hospital treatment of the person concerned nor carried out in his or her interest, and which cause death to or seriously endanger the health of such person or persons;

11. Killing or wounding treacherously individuals belonging to the hostile nation or army;

12. Declaring that no quarter will be given;

13. Destroying or seizing the enemy's property unless such destruction or seizure be imperatively demanded by the necessities of war;

14. Declaring abolished, suspended or inadmissible in a court of law the rights and actions of the nationals of the hostile party;

15. Compelling the nationals of the hostile party to take part in the operations of war directed against their own country, even if they were in the belligerent's service before the commencement of the war;

16. Pillaging a town or place, even when taken by assault; (xvii) Employing poison or poisoned weapons;

17. Employing asphyxiating, poisonous or other gases, and all analogous liquids, materials or devices;

18. Employing bullets which expand or flatten easily in the human body, such as bullets with a hard envelope which does not entirely cover the core or is pierced with incisions;

19. Employing weapons, projectiles and material and methods of warfare which are of a nature to cause superfluous injury or unnecessary suffering or which are inherently indiscriminate in violation of the international law of armed conflict, provided that such weapons, projectiles and material and methods of warfare are the subject of a comprehensive prohibition and are included in an annex to this Statute, by an amendment in accordance with the relevant provisions set forth in articles 121 and 123;

20. Committing outrages upon personal dignity, in particular humiliating and degrading treatment;

21. Committing rape, sexual slavery, enforced prostitution, forced pregnancy, as defined in article 7, paragraph 2 (f), enforced sterilization, or any other form of sexual violence also constituting a grave breach of the Geneva Conventions;

22. Utilizing the presence of a civilian or other protected person to render certain points, areas or military forces immune from military operations;

23. Intentionally directing attacks against buildings, material, medical units and transport, and personnel using the distinctive emblems of the Geneva Conventions in conformity with international law;

24. Intentionally using starvation of civilians as a method of warfare by depriving them of objects indispensable to their survival, including wilfully impeding relief supplies as provided for under the Geneva Conventions;

25. Conscripting or enlisting children under the age of fifteen years into the national armed forces or using them to participate actively in hostilities.

Every belligerent bears responsibility for the conduct of its agents during conflict. Every serviceperson is bound by military law, the law of the country they serve, and domestic law. Any breach may be prosecuted either in the civilian or the military courts. In fact the Geneva Convention requires any signatory to it to enact any legislation that is "necessary to provide effective penal sanctions" for any breaches.

The law also allows the enemy state to prosecute those accused of infraction. Nor does it only affect military personnel. The atrocities of World War II were only possible because of the co-operation of administrators. There is no particular need to prosecute only those at the top of the hierarchy. Low level administrators carrying out the actions of senior judges and cabinet members are as vulnerable to war crimes charges as anybody else. Even the civilian population are under specific duties under Art 17 (1) of the AP/1 to resect the wounded, sick and shipwrecked and there are clear prohibitions in Art 8 (2)(a) (i) of the Rome Statute upon killing or committing acts of pillage.

Individuals

Lawful combatants are entitled to attack lawful targets and would only be vulnerable to prosecution if they exceeded their powers.

Civilians are protected individuals. Unlawful combatants are those that present as a civilian by day, seeking the protections a civilian would enjoy, and engage in the strikes of a soldier by night.

A war criminal is a more complicated animal. Of course, a war criminal need not be a combatant at all. He can be a civilian not engaged in any form of hostility. He can be a lawful combatant who acted in excess of his powers. He may also be an unlawful combatant who engaged in a war crime, for instance, the abuse of flags of surrender.

Jurisdiction

A war criminal can be tried under international law, domestic law, and by the enemy.

An unlawful combatant is not subject to international law unless he commits war crimes. Therefore he can be tried only by the enemy or for breaches of domestic law by the power that he serves.

Defences

It is clearly no defence to say that a crime was committed because orders were being followed. All belligerents, from the General to the footsoldier, have a duty to refuse unlawful orders. However, very junior persons may have mitigation on this basis.

A person ordering a crime, implicitly or explicitly, is considered the main offender using an agent to commit a crime (K. Ambos "Article 25, Commentary on the Rome statute of the international criminal.")

The ICTY Appeals Chamber in *Prosecutor v Kordic et al*, supra note 828, at Para 281 ruled that "ordering" meant use of authority to instruct another to commit an offence.

It is clear that in order need not be given in writing. It can be explicit or implicit and evidenced by circumstantial means (*Prosecutor v Blaskic*, supra note 821, at para 281). Of course, an order that is not given in writing may be harder to prove. Equally, any order may be open to more than one interpretation. A commander may very well defend on the basis that this was a case of unwitting incitement.

Command Responsibility

A commander is responsible for both his orders and his omissions. Clearly a commander would be responsible for order unlawful orders he issues. However, he may also be deemed responsible for the unlawful actions of his men if they can be attributed, even in part, to his failure to perform acts required by international law, for instance, to supervise and punish appropriately.

Indeed, a commander bears a responsibility to supervise the actions of his subordinates. Even if he himself does not issue an unlawful order, there must be in place checks and balances to deal with those who perpetrate war crimes on a frolic of their own.

Equally, a commander can only be liable person if there is a certain dereliction of duty on his part and his subordinates take advantage of that. In the *High Command* case, supra note 1556, at 543 the Tribunal were clear that "the act [must] be directly traceable to him or where his failure to properly supervise his subordinates constitutes criminal negligence on his part".

The current case law of the ICTY makes clear that a commander is accountable for his own failures and his own omissions, but not the autonomous initiatives of subordinates about which he had no influence. The *Krnojelac* judgment made clear that the commanding officer is not charged with the crimes of his subordinates but with his own failure to exercise control.

That said, Art 87.1 of AP/I does impose a positive duty upon States to demand that Commanders "prevent, and where necessary to suppress and to report to competent authorities breaches of the Conventions and of this Protocol".

Art 87.3 of AP/I would appear to remove the discretion of Commanders to do nothing if they saw fit.

CHAPTER NINE
RESPONSIBILITY OF SERVICE PERSONNEL, STATES AND LEGAL ADVISORS

International humanitarian law binds states and individuals from the foot soldier to the general and beyond. Military personnel should be under no illusion; nobody is protected. International law generally only binds the state. Not so with humanitarian law.

An individual soldier who acts contrary to humanitarian law may face criminal consequences. This applies to all ranks as we saw earlier. All members of the armed forces are obliged to comply and ensure compliance with all rules of international humanitarian law binding upon their state.

The duty extends beyond mere compliance. There are positive obligations to ensure that others comply as we saw above under chain of command and criminal consequences for failing to supervise and correct.

Further, the four Geneva Conventions and Protocols oblige all contracting parties to extend the doctrine of the Conventions as widely as possible including encouraging the civilian population of occupied countries to study them.

Instructions to soldiers must be given upon what is or is not lawful by senior officers and legal advisors. Of course, a commander cannot be responsible for controlling every action of his subordinates. But he is responsible for ensuring that forces under his command have the opportunity to be fully acquainted with the law that binds them.

It should also be noted that the type of war does not change the demand that a soldier complies with humanitarian law. It does not matter whether a war is one of national liberation or guerrilla warfare; one situation may be more desperate than the other but that changes no legal requirement.

CHAPTER TEN
JURISDICTION OVER
WAR CRIMES

In principle, jurisdiction is universal. Every state is free to punish any war crime. It matters not that the acts complained of took place outside of its territory or by a person not subject to its rule or were towards a person or group of persons with no link at all to the prosecuting state. All that is required is that is that the accused person is in the custody of the prosecuting state when the matter is brought to trial.

Prosecutions can be very costly and place an onerous burden upon recovering states. Moreover, it relies upon the state in question having a developed and trustworthy legal framework which may not be the case if a nation is recovering from the devastation of war.

While any state may bring a prosecution, in practice it also need not. It is possible to argue that the international community are committed to the prosecution of war crimes but any state has the option either to prosecute themselves or to extradite an offender. Failing that, there is always the option of handing them over to an international tribunal. Either option satisfies the duty. States are not compelled to investigate war crimes, but no state can obstruct. What a state cannot do is protect or harbour an international criminal from prosecution.

International tribunals are very powerful, but they prosecute only a very small percentage. They are really a tool of last resort.

Persons responsible

Any person who commits any war crime is criminally responsible both nationally and internationally. The Nuremberg trials set down that offences contrary to international law are "committed by men, not abstract entities". Some offenders may be placed under huge pressure to commit offences by nefarious regimes and some may just choose to behave badly using his circumstances as a mask for his own venality. In either instance, international law can only be enforced against individuals rather than against states and ideals. The accountability of the individual protects every state and every man.

It is clearly desirable that high ranking officials that commit, order and supervise crime of an international kind should be prosecuted before international tribunals. The public glare, the widespread opprobrium and, indeed, the great assurance of judicial independence are more easily achieved on the international platform. Moreover, there can be certainty that the tribunal complies with human rights standards.

Universality

The original mandate for universal jurisdiction was to deal with piracy. Pirates committed offences on the high seas rather than within the jurisdiction of any state. Mostly this concerned maritime offences against property. The focus has shifted as the world matured. Now international concern is mostly with human rights and basic decency in warfare. The judgment at Nuremberg was a turning point and the consequent adoption of the Geneva Conventions confirmed it. However, nothing imposes an obligation upon a state to exercise international jurisdiction and recovering states would be placed under an unfair burden if required to do so.

On the face of it, jurisdictional issues arise if an offence was committed outside of the territory of the prosecuting state by a person not subject to their jurisdiction. The only real link then is the willingness of that state to bring a prosecution. The principle of universality would allow for this. However, it is more common for states to implement jurisdiction through domestic legislation.

War Crime

This is surprisingly difficult to define. The only thing that is certain is that not every contravention is a war crime. War crimes comprise only the most serious violations of international humanitarian law.

The four Geneva Conventions allowed obliged states to pursue persons said to have committed grave breaches. These states may prosecute or extradite such persons as they wish as long as they do not harbour them.

Article 85 of the Additional Protocol 1 sets down that grave breaches "shall be regarded as war crimes". There are more elaborate tests, but they need not trouble us here.

CHAPTER ELEVEN
ROBOTICS AND DRONES

The onward march of technology continues apace but the principle that men, not machinery, commit offences changes not.

Robotic technology creates special problems for the battlefield. Many remotely controlled weapon systems would be caught by this definition. Most have been accepted into modern forces of long standing. System controllers are often not in direct contact with the weapons and military systems are obtaining increasing autonomy.

Drones are a particularly good example. These devices are widely used for intelligence operations such as surveillance and reconnaissance. Clearly they have benefits. They can fly closer to danger zones without risk to military personnel, and are harder to detect than manned aircraft. The concern is not with unarmed drones. The concern for LOAC lies with the new rising armed drone. Armed drone strikes do blur the boundaries of the battlefield. Historically, operations would be confined to a battlespace. It would be clear what is or is not a legitimate objective and was responsible for any strike. The use of remote aggression by a person outside of the conflict zone is more opaque. Not all operators are military personnel. The US relies upon the CIA to conduct an armed drone programme manned by civilians. This is something they are entitled to do but it does change the status of the operator. A civilian could not enjoy the protected status of the belligerent. Indeed, they may well become direct participants to hostilities with all that implies.

Accountability may be harder to determine. An aircraft system may be either controlled, preprogrammed by the crew or fully autonomous. Even with the autonomous systems, it would be unrealistic to think that humans have no responsibility. Such a system is a device like any other - designed, manufactured and controlled by a human being. However, it may be difficult to allocate responsibility to any particular person. An infanteer who commits war crimes will be easy to identify and will face the consequences. A remote weapons system is not so simple. Remotely piloted vehicles are commanded by an operator and LOAC presumes they have control. Who is to blame if devices malfunction? With fully autonomous systems, there would be no operator in control. The designer and programmer, who will probably both be civilians, may have greater responsibility than the person who switches it on. What then would happen if those persons were based outside the jurisdiction of the belligerent and the conflict zone.

Nanotechnology is a further growth area. Back in 1925 Geneva prohibited the use of "asphyxiating, poisonous … gases" and bacteriological warfare. There were further prohibitions upon biological weapons in 1972 and chemical weapons in 1993. Nanotechnology means the manipulation of material. Chemicals at nanoparticle size can react differently to normal size. They can be used perfectly legitimately as a shield rather than a sword, for instance to enhance the strength of protective vests and body army worn by the military. It would certainly enhance robotic capacity and space technology. When they are used to enhance weapons that are employed aggressively, the considerations are different.

Article 36 of the Additional Protocol I imposes the following obligation:

> "In the study, development, acquisition or adoption of a new weapon, means or method of warfare, a High Contracting Party is under an obligation to determine whether its employment would, in some or all circumstances, be prohibited by this Protocol or by any other

*international law applicable to the High Con-
tracting Party".*

This is so broad in scope that the requirement is for
contracting parties to review every weapon regularly
whether involved in hostility or not.

Rapid development of technology causes concern,
especially amongst academics. Specific regulation
upon cyber combat has been called for and may yet
arrive.

CHAPTER TWELVE
PRIVATE MILITARY SECURITY COMPANIES

The legitimate use of force and aggression is no longer the domain of states. For many reasons, many thousands of private contractors provide military and security services. Many operate in zones of armed conflict, carrying out functions that were traditionally the preserve of service personnel. This may be unpalatable but it is prevalent. Cecile Fabre correctly notes "the prevalent normative view on the marketization of war is that it is morally wrong – for reasons to be found, in part, in the medieval condemnation of mercenarism".

The US Department of defence had more contracted personnel in Afghanistan and Iraq than service personnel.

Combat

This was far more common in the 1990s than now. The British company Sandlin International provided combat services to the governments of Angola and Sierra Leone and were engaged by Papua New Guinea to suppress an uprising.

Some firms were more predisposed to violent conflict than others. Some, such as Aegis, Blackwater, and Erinys were involved in some four hundred incidents but others, such as Crescent, Custer Battles, and Kroll were involved in less than a dozen. That said, studies have found that in every conflict in Iraq that concerned these firms, they used deadly force during their encounters with insurgents less often than their opponents.

Such was the international opprobrium that they were ultimately dissolved and no company will provide offensive combat services on the open market today. However, other areas have boomed.

<u>Security and intelligence expertise</u>

This is relatively uncontroversial. These contractors mostly provide advice and training to those engaged in conflict. They will also provide intelligence services such as satellite and aerial reconnaissance and photograph interpretation.

Such contractors are not authorised to use force or carry weapons and, in many ways, occupy no different position from the auxiliary support staff every military in history has used.

However, there are instances where the law of armed conflict would be engaged. Even this relatively benign contribution to hostilities, an immense impact on warfare could be had. Further, private contractors could find themselves in the position of an unprotected belligerent. For example, a private company engaged to train military forces in a particular discipline, and travelling with that force for that reason, may be placed in a position where they witness conflict. Even though they may not themselves fire weapons, if there were to shout instructions to the force under training who then committed unlawful acts, then the engaging states would be in breach.

For instance, the US outsourced its prisoner interrogation in Iraq. The CACI provided several interrogators work at detention centres in Iraq including the Abu Ghraib prison. One of the things that emerged from the prisoner abuse scandal in 2004 was that 50% of the interrogators involved in the scandal were private contractors. As a result, the US have changed this policy and confine their interrogators solely to members of the armed forces.

Armed Security

Generally this will involve physical protection of persons or property in battle zones. This may involve security escorts of high-ranking individuals, convoy security to protect individuals and property travelling to insecure areas, but far more commonly it would just involve protection of static sites. This would be particularly prevalent in housing areas, reconnaissance areas or municipal buildings.

Such security contractors are entitled to bear arms but there are restrictions upon the type of weapons they can use and operate and they only have authority to use force in self-defence or defence of another. These non-state actors would not be equipped with machine guns, auto-cannons, missiles or tank cannons. Aggressive combat cannot be within their remit and any attempt to deploy it would be a breach. Of course, in high-intensity conflict the distinction between offensive combat and defensive security may become blurred.

Military support

Again, this can involve the type of auxiliary services that every fighting force in history has relied upon. This could include the provision of basic services such as food and water, healthcare, laundry, and also the assembly of military camps and bases. This type of support will be far less controversial than many others.

Challenges and concerns

The main concern is that private security companies are not subject to the same control, training and accountability as military personnel would be. Clearly, private security interrogators hired by the states and used in Abu Ghraib were not subject to adequate screening and had no formal interrogation trading.

Nevertheless, states do have legal obligations to control private security companies and hold them accountable when they act in the field of war. The law provides an obligation to ensure compliance with international humanitarian law and punish breaches.

Also, international human rights law imposes positive obligations upon states to prevent recurring violations, to minimise the risk to life and to protect individuals in custody.

It should also be noted that it is not only the engaging stage that is responsible for breaches. Clearly, the hiring state would be responsible if a contractor acting as its agent engaged in misconduct. Also, an occupying state or a home state would have a positive obligation to punish and control the behaviour of private contractors.

Attempts have been made to regulate the use of private military security but states should not fall into the error of thinking that engaging contractors will protect them from breach. Equally, individuals must not think that their actions are consequence free because they are not members of the armed forces of the power that they serve.

CHAPTER THIRTEEN
SEXUAL VIOLENCE IN CONFLICT

The use of sexual violence as a weapon of war has been prohibited for centuries. It is traceable at least to the 1863 Leiber Code. it is now prohibited by international humanitarian law, international human rights law, international criminal law and the national criminal law in almost every jurisdiction. LOAC is always the starting point. The Geneva Conventions and Protocols, universally recognised by States, specifically prohibit rape in international and non-international conflict. Other sexual offences not amounting to rape or covered either expressly or implicitly.

The UN Security Council Resolution 1325 established what is now known as the "Women, peace and security" agenda. This was unanimously passed through the council in October 2000, the states having been provoked into action by the genocidal rapes of Bosnia only a few years earlier. That Resolution recommended that states draft national action plans although not all states have acted.

Further, Resolution 1325 created a presumption against granting amnesties for sexual crimes. By 2013, and the passage of Resolution 2106, this was strengthened to "the need for the exclusion of sexual violence crime from amnesty provisions" without equivocation. This was the first resolution to mention male survivors and therefore recognise that rape was a weapon that could be used against both men and women.

Clearly rape is something that can take place during conflict and peacetime alike. The concern for LOAC is that rape can be put to use as a weapon of war where perpetrators choose sexual violence as a tactic of terror in the pursuit of wider aims.

A uniformed serviceperson who used sexual violence against civilians or detainees or combatants of any kind would commit a war crime. A superior who ordered him so to do would commit further war crimes as would a superior who knew of the occurrence of sexual offending or of the risk and failed to punish and control.

The more thorny issue is the position of a non-state actor who used sexual violence as a weapon of war. Sexual violence would engage human rights violations. All states would have an obligation to deal with such an abuser. The occupying force would have a responsibility under international human rights law to have in place support measures for complainants and means of controlling abuses. Failing to do so would amount to a breach.

Therefore, it should be noted that any person, regardless of the power that they serve, who used rape as a weapon of war would commit a war crime and could be tried by any state willing to do so.

Sexual violence – a method of torture

The ICTY has developed the law upon sexual violence during armed conflict following the conflicts in Yugoslavia and Rwanda. In the *Akayesu* judgment ICTR 96-4-T the Trial Chamber accepted that rape "in fact constitutes torture when inflicted by or at the instigation of or with the consent or acquiescence of a public official or other person acting in an official capacity".

Sexual violence – genocide

To constitute an act of genocide, sexual violence has to satisfy one of the elements listed in the Convention on the Prevention and Punishment of Crimes of Genocide:

1. Killing members of the group

2. Causing serious bodily or mental harm to members of the group

3. Deliberately inflicting on the group conditions of life calculated to bring about its physical destruction in whole or in part

4. Imposing measures intended to prevent births within the group

5. Forcibly transferring children of the group to another group.

There is no need to show that the act has fully exterminated the group as long as it was done with the specific intent to destroy "in whole or in part".

In the *Akayesu* judgment the Trial Chamber considered the sexual violence targeted towards the Tutsi women and noted that it was "an integral part of the process of destruction, specifically targeting Tutsi women and specifically contributing to their destruction and to the destruction of the Tutsi group as a whole". The Trial Chamber further considered the element of "imposing measures intended to prevent births within the group" and determined that this should be construed as sexual mutilation, sterilisation, forced birth control, segregation of the sexes, and prohibitions upon marriage.

Sexual violence - enslavement

In the case of *Foca* (The Hague) 12 June 2002, the three accused were said to have detained the victims and forced them to perform household chores and raped them repeatedly.

The Trial Chamber defined enslavement as "the exercise of any or all of the powers attaching to the right of ownership over a person". It went on to assert that under this definition "enslavement include(s) elements of control and ownership; the restriction or control of an individual's autonomy, freedom of choice or freedom of movement".

It is submitted that to reach this hurdle there must be some form of detention as well as sexual violence.

CHAPTER FOURTEEN
LIABILITY FOR THE
ACTIONS OF ALLIES

Cooperation among states in the course of conflict is becoming extremely and increasingly commonplace. Coalitions of states are now the norm. This is certainly been true of the recent conflict in the Middle East.

Such cooperation has many advantages. The free world can assist each other as a matter of operational law. However, it does beg the question of where the assisting state would be left if their help contributed to a breach of international law.

The current law arises from the "Articles on the Responsibility of States for Internationally Wrongful Acts", hereafter the "Articles on State Responsibility". Article 16 provides that:

> *"A State which aids or assists another State in the commission of the internationally wrongful act by the latter is internationally responsible for doing so if:*

I.a.i.1. that State does so with knowledge of the circumstances of the internationally wrongful act; and

I.a.i.2. the act would be internationally wrongful if committed by that stage"

Put simply, an assisting state should not assist another to do anything that it would not be allowed by international law to do itself.

Some guidance is provided by the International Law Commission's, hereafter the ILC, Commentary to the Articles which set down three conditions circumscribing the scope of responsibility. Firstly the assisting state must be aware the circumstances making the conduct of the assisted State unlawful. The intention of the ILC was not to make an otherwise compliant state responsible for the actions of the state that goes rogue with no warning. Secondly, the aid or assistance must be given in order to facilitate the commission of that act and must actually do so. Thirdly, they completed act must be one that would be unlawful if committed by the assisting state itself.

Article 16 does not define "aid or assistance". Clearly, it would affect a broad range of activity. The supply of weapons, the handing over of detainees questioning, the provision of logistical assistance and simply financial support could be included. Already, there have been calls by Parliamentary select committee for the government of the UK to suspend arms supply to Saudi Arabia that will be used in air strikes against the rebels in Yemen. That also led to a High Court challenge from the Campaign Against Arms Trade group that, at the time of writing, has not concluded.

It must be actual aid or assistance. Mere encouragement would not offend, although incitement may be caught by other rules of law.

There must also be a nexus between the assistance provided and the internationally wrongful act that is the cause of complaint. A state can only be responsible for the extent that its own conduct has caused the act. While the guidance from the ILC does set down that the aid or assistance need not have been essential to the performance of the act, it goes on to say that it must have "contributed significantly". Later the ICL does say that the aid need only have contributed to a "minor degree" which is contradictory, but it is clear that there must be some causative connection.

The ultimate act of international role must be also be unlawful if committed by the assisting state. It would seem that the purpose of this Article is to prevent the state complying with international law by not acting directly but lending support to a state or counterterrorism group that is willing to act at variance. This may be very relevant where one state is bound by human rights treaty obligations, such as the UK, and another is not, such as the US.

Responsibility under Article 16 is not for the internationally wrongful act itself however. It is for the act of assisting. Nevertheless the ancillary responsibility will be aggravated by the gravity of the act that it assists.

Specific rules governing the issue of aiding and assisting had already existed in international law. The rules of LOAC will always be primary. It is only a state act inconsistently with those rules that the secondary rules of state responsibility under the Articles are engaged. Agents of the state should also be aware that they may face individual responsibility for any rogue assistance provided.

There remains a substantial amount of doubt over the interpretation of Article 16. There is a lack of case law in this area.

Of course, in a global economy we cannot hide from the fact that there must be international cooperation and some states have a record of better compliance with LOAC than others. However, states that provide assistance to rogue states would be at risk of prosecution themselves.

The risk can be mitigated by proper assessment of the risks of providing assistance which is reviewed regularly. After all, the provision of weapons for offensive combat may not offend if the combat, at the time of sale, was a lawful one. If the conduct of the warring state changed during the course of conflict and those weapons were used in flagrant breach of the law then the decision to provide assistance thereafter would need to be revisited. If it is not, their liability arises.

CHAPTER FIFTEEN
COUNTERMEASURES

Countermeasures create a unique problem. An injured state is entitled to act in reprisal. However, this would mean acting in a way that would otherwise be contrary to the international obligations of the injured state. There are, therefore, conditions that must be satisfied before self-help can be used and severe limitations upon its use, not least because countermeasures have the potential for abuse in particular where there is inequality between the injured state and the responsible state.

Statute and the decisions of international tribunals alike recognise that countermeasures are justified in some circumstances. Article 23 deals with countermeasures in response to internationally wrongful acts.

Countermeasures have been interpreted to mean some form of strike. It is important to understand that they do not mean unfriendly conduct towards the responsible state. For whatever reason and whatever their motives, a state is entitled to act in retorsion if this act does not amount to something that would breach LOAC if it were not in circumstances of injury. Limitations upon normal diplomatic relationships, trade embargoes and withdrawal of voluntary aid are all open to a state without the satisfaction of any conditions.

Countermeasures are limited by the requirement that they be directed at the responsible stage rather than at third parties (Art 49, paras 1 and 2). Of course, that does not mean that they cannot incidentally affect the position of other states and countries. In a global economy, commonly there would be some neutral consequences. Suspension of any trade agreements may well affect third party states. These are indirect effects which are lawful and cannot be avoided.

Countermeasures must be proportionate (Art 51). This is, as ever, an elastic term but it is one that must be considered. However badly a rogue state has behaved or continues to behave, that does not mean that it has made itself a target for any combination of countermeasures regardless of severity.

This was fairly heavily considered in the *Air Service Agreement* arbitration. This case involved the French refusal to allow a change of gauge in London on flights from the US and the countermeasure of the US to suspend Air France flights to Los Angeles altogether. This was held to be reasonable because it did not appear to be a disproportionate action compared to that taken by France. The majority dictum is important though. The majority view was that "all counter measures must [...] have some degree of equivalence with the alleged breach [...] It has been observed, generally, that judging the "proportionality" of countermeasures is not an easy task and can best be accomplished by approximation". They must also obviously not be a breach of any basic obligations (Art 50, para 1).

Countermeasures cannot be taken by an injured state before it warns the responsible state under Article 52. This Article lays down procedural conditions that must be taken before an injured state can resort to countermeasures. It lays down:

1. *Before taking countermeasures, an injured State shall:*

   a) *Call upon the responsible State, in accordance with article 43, to fulfil its obligations under Part Two*

   b) *Notify the responsible State of any decision to take countermeasures and offer to negotiate with that State*

2. *Notwithstanding paragraph 1(b) the injured State may take such urgent countermeasures as are necessary to preserve its rights.*

3. *Countermeasures may not be taken, and is already taken must be suspended without undue delay if;*

    a) *the intentionally wrongful act has ceased; and*

    b) *the dispute is pending before court or tribunal which has the authority to make decisions binding on the parties.*

4. *Paragraph 3 does not apply if the responsible State fails to implement the dispute settlement procedures in good faith.*

Overall, this Article seeks to establish reasonable conditions to avoid the need for aggression. At the same time it takes into account the possibility that some form of self-help maybe immediately required and that some disputes may be settled by arbitration.

The controversy has made in the requirement under Paragraph 1(b) to notify the responsible state of any decision to strike. Arguably, this places an already injured state at a further disadvantage. From the point of view of world peace though, this gives a target state an option to address its offending conduct. Also this is mitigated by paragraph 2 which allows urgent countermeasures. These are obviously designed to address a situation where an offending state may seek to immunise itself against countermeasures using the notification period. Immediate action may include things such as the freezing temporarily assets of the responsible state within the jurisdiction of the injured state.

Paragraph 3 addresses situations where the wrongful act has ceased and the dispute is submitted to the court or tribunal. It is quite clear that in such a case countermeasures must stop for as long as the dispute settlement procedure takes. If countermeasures have already been taken then they must be suspended "without delay".

The growing global practice of cooperation and coalitions does create controversy in this area. It creates a position where one state may take countermeasures on behalf of an injured state. It is clear in Article 48, para 1, that any state has the right to take lawful measures to bring about the end of unlawful action by a belligerent state.

The conditions that must be met before countermeasures are appropriate are defined in case law and they are not complicated: "In the first place must be taken in response to a previous international wrongful act of another state and must be directed against that state" (*Gabcikovo-Nagymaros Project (Hungary/Slovakia).*

Article 49, para 1 sets down that there is an objective standard for the taking of countermeasures and further makes clear that countermeasures must be the purposes of inducing a belligerent state to do something it must stop doing something it must not. It is a brave state that would take countermeasures upon its unilateral assessment of the situation. It may find itself before a tribunal for its own conduct. This is especially the case if the balance of power between the regulating stage and the belligerent state is great.

Countermeasures must be temporary (Art 49, paras 2, 3 and 53). The purpose of countermeasures is to enforce compliance with international obligations. Revenge strikes are strictly prohibited. If a rogue state stops misbehaving and ensures reparations then the need for countermeasures comes to an end.

However, it is clear that countermeasures need not stop merely because the responsible state has stopped committing internationally wrongful acts. The primary purpose of counter strikes is to enforce compliance but there can be greater demands. Under Article 30 the responsible state is under an obligation to stop committing acts of international wrong but also to "offer appropriate assurances and guarantees of non-repetition, if circumstances so require" (Article 30 (b)). In most circumstances, satisfaction of this kind could only be symbolic and may not, per se, justify a further strike when the proportionality principle of Art 51 is applied.

Also, Article 31 sets down that:

1. The responsible state is under an obligation to make full reparation for the injury caused by the internationally wrongful act.

2. Injury includes any damage, whether material or moral, caused by the internationally wrongful act of a State

Reparation can obviously allow an injured state to take greater action although that would need to be filtered through the prism of proportionality. The difficulty is that without this measure a rogue State would be indemnified against countermeasures as long as the unlawful conduct had ceased.

Article 50 provides comprehensive guidance upon the obligations that must not be affected by countermeasures. It sets down:

1. Counter measures shall not affect:

   a) the obligation to refrain from the threat or use of force as embodied in the Charter of the United Nations;

   b) obligations for the protection of fundamental human rights;

   c) obligations of the humanitarian character prohibiting reprisals;

   d) other obligations under peremptory norms of general international law

2. A State taking countermeasures is not relieved from fulfilling its obligations;

    a) under any dispute settlement procedure applicable between it and the responsible State

    b) to respect the inviolability of diplomatic or consular agents, premises, archives and documents.

Obligations may not be impaired by countermeasures. An injured state, however objectionable it may be, is required to continue to respect these obligations. They are fairly fundamental and would be sacrosanct under other rules of law as they go to primary obligations. A breach of any of the obligations under part one would be objectionable under LOAC.

Countermeasures that seem innocuous may be offences. Economic sanctions, on the face of it, seem to be something an injured state is entirely within its rights to use. However, the effect upon civilians must be considered, in particular children. Paragraph 1 of Article 54 of the Additional Protocol to the Geneva conventions of 12 August 1949 stipulate without equivocation that "starvation of civilians as a method of warfare is prohibited".

Paragraph 1(d) prohibits any countermeasure that affects obligations under "peremptory norms" of international law. This would include any action caught by any of the other sub paragraphs and also anything else prohibited. States may also agree between themselves upon additional rules of international law which may not be the subject of countermeasures and that would be caught by this paragraph. The European Union treaties are a prime example. Paragraph (1)(d) has been considered by caselaw. In *Prosecutor v Zoran Kupreskic, Mirjian Kupreski, Vlatko Jupreskic, Drago Josipovic, Dragan Papic, Vladmire Santic ("Lasva Valley")* it was interpreted to prohibit "the reprisal killing of innocent persons, more or less chosen at random, without any requirement or guilty or any form of a trial".

Part two of Article 50 is clearly defined to leave open the lines of diplomatic communication allowing for the conflict come to an end. An injured State would be entitled to recall ambassadors as there is specific provision for that in the Vienna Convention on Diplomatic Relations. Also it may suspend diplomatic relations. These do not amount to improper countermeasures or countermeasures at all. What must be protected is the physical safety of diplomatic agents, their premises and documents. To do otherwise would render them resident hostages. This would have the effect of undermining the entire institution of diplomacy.

MORE BOOKS BY
LAW BRIEF PUBLISHING

A selection of our other titles available now:-

'A Practical Guide to Immigration Law and Tier 1 Entrepreneur Applications' by Sarah Pinder
'A Practical Guide to Unlawful Eviction and Harassment' by Stephanie Lovegrove
'In My Backyard! A Practical Guide to Neighbourhood Plans' by Dr Sue Chadwick
'A Practical Guide to the Law Relating to Food' by Ian Thomas
'A Practical Guide to the Ending of Assured Shorthold Tenancies' by Elizabeth Dwomoh
'Commercial Mediation – A Practical Guide' by Nick Carr
'A Practical Guide to Financial Services Claims' by Chris Hegarty
'The Law of Houses in Multiple Occupation: A Practical Guide to HMO Proceedings' by Julian Hunt

'A Practical Guide to Unlawful Eviction and Harassment' by Stephanie Lovegrove

'A Practical Guide to Solicitor and Client Costs' by Robin Dunne

'Artificial Intelligence – The Practical Legal Issues' by John Buyers

'A Practical Guide to Wrongful Conception, Wrongful Birth and Wrongful Life Claims' by Rebecca Greenstreet

'Occupiers, Highways and Defective Premises Claims: A Practical Guide Post-Jackson – 2nd Edition' by Andrew Mckie

'A Practical Guide to Financial Ombudsman Service Claims' by Adam Temple & Robert Scrivenor

'A Practical Guide to the Law of Enfranchisement and Lease Extension' by Paul Sams

'A Practical Guide to Marketing for Lawyers – 2nd Edition' by Catherine Bailey & Jennet Ingram

'A Practical Guide to Advising Schools on Employment Law' by Jonathan Holden

'Certificates of Lawful Use and Development: A Guide to Making and Determining Applications' by Bob Mc Geady & Meyric Lewis

'A Practical Guide to the Law of Dilapidations' by Mark Shelton

'A Practical Guide to the 2018 Jackson Personal Injury and Costs Reforms' by Andrew Mckie

'A Guide to Consent in Clinical Negligence Post-Montgomery' by Lauren Sutherland QC

'A Practical Guide to Running Housing Disrepair and Cavity Wall Claims: 2nd Edition' by Andrew Mckie & Ian Skeate

'A Practical Guide to the General Data Protection Regulation (GDPR)' by Keith Markham

'A Practical Guide to Digital and Social Media Law for Lawyers' by Sherree Westell

'A Practical Guide to Holiday Sickness Claims – 2nd Edition' by Andrew Mckie & Ian Skeate

'A Practical Guide to Inheritance Act Claims by Adult Children Post-Ilott v Blue Cross' by Sheila Hamilton Macdonald

'A Practical Guide to Elderly Law' by Justin Patten

'Arguments and Tactics for Personal Injury and Clinical Negligence Claims' by Dorian Williams

'A Practical Guide to QOCS and Fundamental Dishonesty' by James Bentley

'A Practical Guide to Drone Law' by Rufus Ballaster, Andrew Firman, Eleanor Clot

'Practical Mediation: A Guide for Mediators, Advocates, Advisers, Lawyers, and Students in Civil, Commercial, Business, Property, Workplace, and Employment Cases'
by Jonathan Dingle with John Sephton

'Practical Horse Law: A Guide for Owners and Riders' by Brenda Gilligan

'A Comparative Guide to Standard Form Construction and Engineering Contracts'
by Jon Close

'A Practical Guide to Compliance for Personal Injury Firms Working With Claims Management Companies' by Paul Bennett

'A Practical Guide to the Landlord and Tenant Act 1954: Commercial Tenancies'
by Richard Hayes & David Sawtell

'A Practical Guide to Personal Injury Claims Involving Animals' by Jonathan Hand

'A Practical Guide to Psychiatric Claims in Personal Injury' by Liam Ryan

'Introduction to the Law of Community Care in England and Wales' by Alan Robinson

'A Practical Guide to Dog Law for Owners and Others' by Andrea Pitt

'Ellis and Kevan on Credit Hire – 5th Edition' by Aidan Ellis & Tim Kevan

'RTA Allegations of Fraud in a Post-Jackson Era: The Handbook – 2nd Edition' by Andrew Mckie

'RTA Personal Injury Claims: A Practical Guide Post-Jackson' by Andrew Mckie

'On Experts: CPR35 for Lawyers and Experts' by David Boyle

'An Introduction to Personal Injury Law' by David Boyle

'A Practical Guide to Claims Arising From Accidents Abroad and Travel Claims' by Andrew Mckie & Ian Skeate

'A Practical Guide to Cosmetic Surgery Claims' by Dr Victoria Handley

'A Practical Guide to Chronic Pain Claims'
by Pankaj Madan

'A Practical Guide to Claims Arising from Fatal
Accidents' by James Patience

'A Practical Approach to Clinical Negligence Post-
Jackson' by Geoffrey Simpson-Scott

'A Practical Guide to Personal Injury Trusts'
by Alan Robinson

'Employers' Liability Claims: A Practical Guide
Post-Jackson' by Andrew Mckie

'A Practical Guide to Subtle Brain Injury Claims'
by Pankaj Madan

'The Law of Driverless Cars: An Introduction'
by Alex Glassbrook

'A Practical Guide to Personal Injuries in Sport' by
Adam Walker & Patricia Leonard

'A Practical Guide to Costs in Personal Injury
Cases' by Matthew Hoe

'The No Nonsense Solicitors' Practice: A Guide To
Running Your Firm' by Bettina Brueggemann

'A Practical Guide to Alternative Dispute Resolution in Personal Injury Claims – Getting the Most Out of ADR Post-Jackson' by Peter Causton, Nichola Evans, James Arrowsmith

'Baby Steps: A Guide to Maternity Leave and Maternity Pay' by Leah Waller

'The Queen's Counsel Lawyer's Omnibus: 20 Years of Cartoons from The Times 1993-2013' by Alex Steuart Williams

These books and more are available to order online direct from the publisher at www.lawbriefpublishing.com, where you can also read free sample chapters. For any queries, contact us on 0844 587 2383 or mail@lawbriefpublishing.com.

Our books are also usually in stock at www.amazon.co.uk with free next day delivery for Prime members, and at good legal bookshops such as Hammicks and Wildy & Sons.

We are regularly launching new books in our series of practical day-to-day practitioners' guides. Visit our website and join our free newsletter to be kept informed and to receive special offers, free chapters, etc.

You can also follow us on Twitter at www.twitter.com/lawbriefpub.

www.ingramcontent.com/pod-product-compliance
Lightning Source LLC
Chambersburg PA
CBHW071203200326
41519CB00018B/5351